BEAUTIFUL

Melbourne

BEAUTIFUL
Melbourne

*As night slowly approaches, Melbourne's city lights cast a
glow of tranquility on the city's many changing facades.
Behind these, one can discover an immense variety of restaurants,
nightclubs and theatres, all fulfilling Melbourne's insatiable
desire for enjoyment and entertainment, giving it a style like that
of no other city.*

Above: *The Melbourne International Festival of the Arts is only one of several festivals that take place every year. Some 3000 artists from all over the world give 500 performances in a host of venues including Botanica, a conservatory-like structure erected specially for the festival in Queen Victoria Gardens near the Arts Centre.*

Opposite, top: *One of the public sculptures to be found at Southgate, a dining and leisure complex on the banks of the Yarra River.*

Opposite, bottom: *The distinctive 115 metre lattice spire of the Arts Centre makes an unmistakable landmark over the Yarra River, just across from the city centre. The Victorian Arts Centre is the hub of the Melbourne arts district, its steel and aluminium spire a guiding beacon. The Centre contains a 2000-seat theatre, a concert hall which holds an audience of 2500, and the National Gallery of Victoria.*

Opposite: *Melbourne, not without justification, considers itself the cultural capital of Australia. The Princess Theatre, built in 1886, is itself worthy of applause, with its elaborate facade and gilded interior with flying cherubs and ornate plasterwork.*

Above: *The Studio is an exciting concept in the Arts Centre, being able to cater for performances in the round, multimedia or multi-screen presentations, or even exhibitions.*

Right: *The National Gallery of Victoria houses a collection of world standing, made up of both European masters and important Australian works.*

Left: *A quiet corner of the Royal Botanic Gardens, 35 hectares of lawns and lakes, tall trees and flower beds, but less than 2 kilometres from the city centre. The world-renowned gardens, begun in the 1840s, contain more than 60 000 plant species from all over the world.*

Bottom left: *The proposal to build a conservatory in Fitzroy Gardens in the 1920s brought howls of protest. Today, however, the building is enjoyed by thousands of people each year.*

Opposite, top: *The floral clock in Queen Victoria Gardens keeps the time for the tens of thousands of people who each day pass along busy St Kilda Road. The design is changed four times a year, using 30 000 flowers.*

Opposite, bottom: *William Guilfoyle, director of the Royal Botanic Gardens for almost 40 years and a brilliant landscaper, understood the use of water in his art, and lakes and tranquil pools take up more than 10 per cent of the gardens.*

Above: *The tranquility of the cityscape at night disguises the flurry of social activity that is occurring within its heart. Much of Melbourne's socialising is centred on its diverse array of over 2500 top quality restaurants.*

Above: *St Kilda's first wine bar, The Dogs Bar, has kept its character and even its fireplace, and still holds appeal for generations both young and old.*
Below: *A strong Jewish community has lived in St Kilda almost since the suburb began. Acland Street has built up a reputation over the years for its cake shops and delicatessens.*
Left: *St Kilda Pier is the best known in Melbourne. It was wooden for many decades, but has been replaced by a more modern* *structure. However, it is still the Pier, and few visitors can resist a casual stroll along it.*
Opposite, top: *Melbourne's market tradition is alive and strong on Sundays at St Kilda Upper Esplanade, which is lined with stallholders selling their handmade wares and crafts.*

Above: *Fans pack the Melbourne Cricket Ground at night to watch their favourite football teams. The ground hosted the first cricket test between Australia and England in 1877 and the long tradition of cricket test series continues here every summer. Melbourne is the birthplace of the unique brand of football, Australian Rules, and the annual grand final is held here to capacity crowds.*

Left: *This is where the hearts beat and the crowds roar – the vast bowl of the Melbourne Cricket Ground, scene of the 1956 Olympiad, which can accommodate 100 000 spectators. Melbourne is acknowledged to be sports crazy, so it is only fitting it has Australia's largest sports stadium. Sports fixtures in the city draw bigger crowds than anywhere else in the country.*

Opposite, top: *Philosophical punters consider what might have been among the debris of their hopes at Flemington Racecourse after the running of the Melbourne Cup, the race that brings the nation to a halt for three minutes on the first Tuesday of every November.*

Opposite, bottom: *Sailboarding in the sunset. Enthusiasts catch a light evening breeze off St Kilda, the ever-popular beach only 5 kilometres from the city centre.*

Opposite, top: *Melbourne's distinguished public and commercial buildings of the nineteenth century, such as the General Post Office, were funded by the fabulous riches of the Victorian goldfields.*

Opposite, bottom: *The Museum of Victoria started in 1854 as a small public collection of minerals and natural science specimens. It now houses over 16 million objects, including the world's finest and largest collection of Aboriginal artefacts. The statue is of Supreme Court Judge Sir Redmond Barry who, in 1880, sentenced bushranger Ned Kelly to death, and himself died two weeks after the hanging.*

Right: *Rowers pass under Princes Bridge against a modern city skyline, whose angular shapes are in sharp contrast to the graceful nineteenth century dome of Flinders Street railway station.*

Below: *Trams are a crucial part of Melbourne's charm and fabric, and have been since 1885. Visitors find they are not only a good way to see the city, the ride itself is a novelty. In the background is Melbourne's Town Hall, with its distinctive tower.*

Below: *Everything about Melbourne Central shopping centre, the city's main covered retail centre, is over the top. It cost $1.2 billion to build, and has more than 150 shops with a combined floorspace of about seven football fields. The oversize pocket watch produces marionette musicians and mechanical Australian birds on the hour, accompanied by a three-minute rendition of 'Waltzing Matilda.'*

Right: *Chapel Street in Prahran has become home to some of Australia's most exciting fashion designers.*

Opposite, bottom: *Amongst the multitude of Sunday markets, Collins Place, at the eastern end of the city centre, draws crowds of enthusiastic shoppers and sightseers hunting for a bargain.*

Above: *Waves of Italian migrants arriving in Melbourne after World War II adopted the suburb of Carlton as their own, particularly Lygon Street, which is today the lively centre of Italian cuisine and culture.*

Opposite, top: *Eight million people are said to visit the Southgate complex every year to enjoy its shops, waterfront cafes and mouth-watering food centres. Many include a relaxing cruise on the Yarra River in their day's plans.*

Opposite, bottom: *Melburnians embrace the cafe lifestyle in Brunswick Street, Fitzroy, a cosmopolitan, out-of-the-ordinary village within a city.*

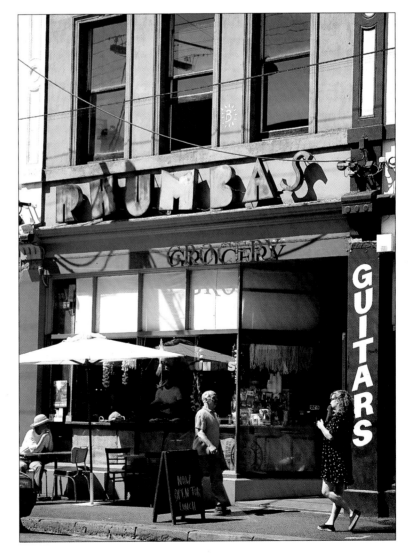

By the Seaside

Opposite, top: *Beaches are only a few minutes by tram from the city centre. Brighton is one of the closest and most popular.*

Opposite, bottom: *Yachts racing off St Kilda against the backdrop of the 2.5 kilometre West Gate Bridge, scene of one of Australia's worst tragedies. A span collapsed during construction in 1970 and 35 workers were killed.*

Above: *Beach huts, known in Melbourne as bathing boxes, are now protected by the National Trust. They are a tradition of the bayside suburbs going back to at least early this century and some have been in the same family for generations.*

🇦🇺 Left: *Victorian men and women who died in two world wars are honoured at the Shrine of Remembrance in Kings Domain, just off busy St Kilda Road.*

Opposite, bottom: *The majestic Shrine of Remembrance is strategically sited so that war veterans marching every Anzac Day to remember Australia's war dead can see it every step of the way from the city centre.*

Right: *An example of the artistic licence in evidence among the public sculpture at Southgate, which is also a favourite place for street performers.*

Below: *A legacy of Melbourne's riches from Victorian times, Rippon Lea is known for its flamboyant style, particularly its iron port-cochere and conservatory. Peacocks roam the gardens.*

Opposite, top: *Flinders Street railway station is a splendid salute to the era of steam trains. It has been the hub of the city's extensive rail system since 1854 and, down the years, a traditional meeting place.*
Opposite, bottom: *Melbourne has more than 3000 restaurants serving more than 70 cuisines.*

Below: *A city garlanded with light lies at the feet of the Rialto Towers, Melbourne's tallest building. The complex is a member of the World Federation of Great Towers.*

Left: *Melburnians love a bargain and the city's markets surpass any others in Australia. The Queen Victoria Market sprawls over 7 hectares and houses more than 1000 traders. The quaint shops along Victoria Street have been beautifully restored.*

Right: *Queen Victoria Market is only one of a number in Melbourne. It was established in 1859, making it the oldest market in the city. Underneath its canopies shoppers can buy anything from fresh produce to unique gifts.*

Bottom, right: *Melburnians love to relax and socialise outdoors. The new riverfront development of Southgate incorporates a hotel, food court, restaurants, cafes, bars and art galleries in the heart of the city's arts and leisure precinct.*

Above: *A business lunch with a Mediterranean flavour. Where better than one of the many outdoor restaurants in Melbourne's Little Italy, Carlton's Lygon Street.*
Opposite, top: *Williamstown has a very strong village atmosphere, and locals still find time for a leisurely cup of coffee and a chat.*
Opposite, bottom: *Fitzroy is the bohemian suburb of Melbourne, known for its vigorous subcultures and comedy theatres and restaurants. And you never know who you will bump into in the street.*

Left: *Melbourne is a shoppers' paradise. In the sprawling Melbourne Central retail complex shopping is an experience, with a touch of extravagance. The hub of the centre is a massive glass cone, which contains a restored historic shot tower.*

Above: *Melbourne is chock-full of eating places. This cafe is in the sunken courtyard of Melbourne Central shopping centre, at the foot of the restored shot tower.*

Opposite: *Melbourne has a number of handsome arcades, the oldest of which is the Royal Arcade, which dates from 1869. Every hour, the giant statues of the legendary figures Gog and Magog strike the time.*

Above: *The Exhibition Building in Carlton Gardens was the largest construction in Melbourne when it was built for the Great Exhibition of 1880. Many of the trees in the surrounding gardens were planted at that time. The city stretches its legs in more than 3000 hectares of parks and gardens, and there are several beautiful, large gardens on the fringe of the rectangle that contains the city centre.*

Opposite, top: *The Exhibition Building had its most glorious moment in 1901 when it was the setting for the ceremonial opening of the first Commonwealth Parliament. Although now reduced to a main hall, it is still used for shows and exhibitions.*

Opposite, bottom: *Australia was ruled from Victoria's Parliament House between Federat 1901 and the Commonwealth Government m Canberra in 1927. The building is the epitom nineteenth century civic architecture.*

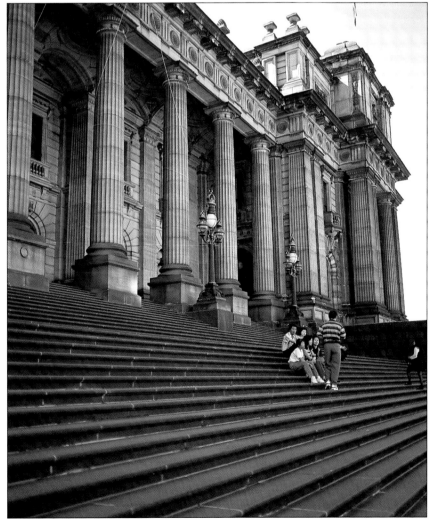

Left: *Melbourne is the only city in Australia to have kept its trams. One has even been restored and transformed into a restaurant which takes diners on a tour of city streets in plush Victorian glory.*

Above: *Melbourne city centre is laid out in an orderly grid system, which makes it convenient for visitors to use the city circle tram service that runs around the perimeter. They can get on and off as often as they like, and the trips are free. The service uses historic trams, painted a distinctive burgundy and cream.*

Left: *Melbourne has forged ahead with the times in its architecture, but has retained its value of the past. Florid ornamentation of a century-old office building now converted into a hotel contrasts with the unadorned lines of Rialto Towers.*

Above: *The heart of Melbourne is one large shopping centre, and no complex is bigger than Melbourne Central. The complex contains Australia's first Japanese department store, Daimaru, and even the nearby railway station is named after it.*

Right: *The Windsor doesn't need stars. In all its Victorian elegance and charm, it is Australia's last deluxe hotel in the truly grand manner. It has recently been beautifully restored to the glories of its golden past.*

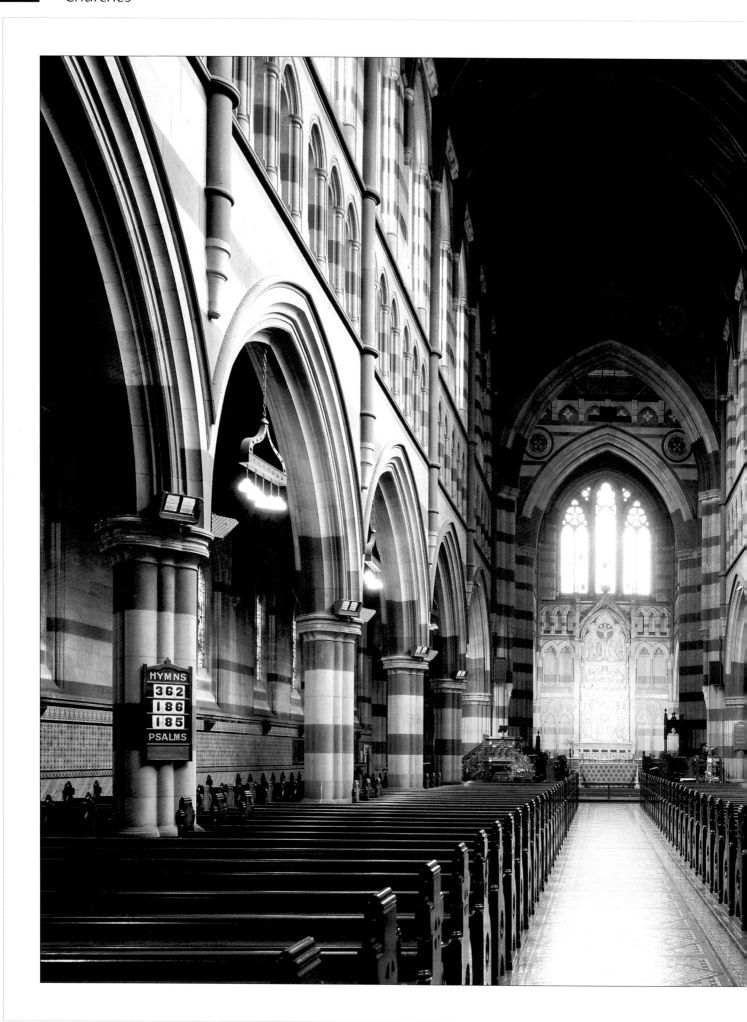

Left: *Australia's largest cathedral, St Patrick's Catholic Cathedral is an outstanding celebration of Gothic Revival architecture. The church is a minor basilica, a status enjoyed by few cathedrals.*

Above: *St Paul's Anglican Cathedral is another magnificent Gothic Revival building. This city landmark was built on the site of an 1850s parish church, and some of the original pews are still in use.*

Below: *The Great Western Window of St Patrick's Cathedral is one of Australia's best examples of stained glass craftsmanship.*

Above: *Melbourne's earliest link with its colonial heritage is the stone cottage of the parents of explorer Captain James Cook, who first landed in Australia in south-east Victoria in 1770. The cottage was shipped from Yorkshire in 1935 and re-erected in an English setting in Fitzroy Gardens to commemorate Melbourne's centenary.*

Opposite, top: *Melbourne has been strolling along St Kilda Pier for years, and still has not tired of it. There is even the traditional wooden pavilion.*

Opposite, bottom: *Species of parrots live i[...] Australia's rainforests, deserts, plains and c[...] even in the gardens of the Royal Melbourne [...]*

Opposite, top: *The grim confines of Old Melbourne Gaol were the scene of 104 hangings, including that of Ned Kelly, Australia's best-known bushranger. The building, now belonging to the National Trust, stands testimony to Victoria's often violent history.*

Opposite, bottom: *Rich rural land owners, known as the "squattocracy", built themselves lavish town residences in the second half of the nineteenth century. One of the most distinguished mansions is Como House, now a National Trust property, which is open to the public.*

Above: *The splendid reading room in the State Library is similar in design and dimension to its counterpart in the British Museum in London. The library opened in 1856 and contains valuable state archives and almost a million volumes.*

Left: *The city skyline as seen across the waters of Port Phillip Bay from Williamstown, Melbourne's salty, maritime suburb of boatyards and ship chandlers, jetties and fishing nets, and a naval dockyard.*

Above: *The palatial 200-room Government House, official residence of the Governor of Victoria, sits serenely among public gardens, yet almost within earshot of the roar of Melbourne's soaring city centre.*

Opposite top: *The high-rise of Melbourne's central business district as seen from Princes Bridge. The city's tallest building, Rialto Towers, is on the left. Melbourne is a vibrant commercial centre, home to many of Australia's leading business institutions.*

Opposite bottom: *Strolling along the banks of the Yarra River is a popular Melbourne pastime, and a footbridge conveniently links Flinders Walk and Southbank Promenade in the shadow of the city centre.*

Above: *Few things are more Australian than the kookaburra, whose distinctive call has been described as ''a raucous high-pitched trilling howl''. This gimlet-eyed ''kooka'' is a resident in the Royal Melbourne Zoo, the world's third oldest zoo.*

Published by New Holland Publishers (Australia), an imprint of National Book Distributors Pty Ltd
3/2 Aquatic Drive, Frenchs Forest, New South Wales, 2086, Australia

First edition 1995
Text © Bob Wilson

Design concept Neville Poulter
Design and DTP Arne Falkenmire
Cartography Globetrotter Travel Map
Editor Katie Millar

Reproduction by Hirt & Carter (Pty) Ltd, Cape Town
Printed and bound by Kyodo Printing Co (Pte) Ltd, Singapore

National Library of Australia
Cataloguing-in-Publication-data

Beautiful Melbourne

ISBN 1 86436 080 1

1. Melbourne (Vic.) — Pictorial works. I. Wilson, Robert.

994.5100222

Photographs:

Roger du Buisson
p 10–11.

National Book Publishers Image Library
front cover (main picture), front cover (left inset), p 1, p 2–3, p 4–5, p 6–7, p 8, p 9 (bottom), p 14–15 (top, right), (bottom, right), (bottom, left), p 16–17, p 18, p 20–21, p 22, (top), p 23, p 24–25, p 26 (top), p 27, p 28–29, p 30, p 31, (top), p 32–33, p 34–35, p 36, p 38–39, p 40–41, p 42, p 43 (bottom), p 44–45, p 47, p 48, back cover, title page.

Tourism Victoria Photographic Library
front cover (right inset), p 9 (top), p 12–13, p 14–15 (top, left), p 19, p 22, (bottom), p 26, (bottom), p 31, (bottom), p 37, p 43 (top), p 46.